World Trivia Questions

Fun Facts About Movies, Art, Animals, TV, Music And Much More

Michelle L. Fischer

Table of Contents

Bluesource And Friends

This book is brought to you by Bluesource And Friends, a happy book publishing company.

Our motto is **"Happiness Within Pages"**.

We promise to deliver amazing value to readers with our books.

We also appreciate honest book reviews from our readers.

Connect with us on our Facebook page www.facebook.com/bluesourceandfriends and stay tuned to our latest book promotions and free giveaways.

Don't forget to claim your FREE book

https://tinyurl.com/karenbrainteasers

Also check out our best seller book

https://tinyurl.com/lateralthinkingpuzzles

Introduction

Welcome to the wonderful world of fun facts, trivia, and interesting things to know about all the things in the world. I have included interesting things about animals that are lesser known, to random facts and details that you wouldn't probably know prior to reading this book. There are so many things that are listed in this book that you should have no problem joining a trivia group at your local bar.

I included information about Presidents, countries, mountains, food, actors, activists, animals, authors, television, movies, music, and even art. This book is so in-depth that you will definitely learn something that was not previously known. I hope this book is enjoyable for you to read and brings you lots of inspiration.

Chapter 1: What you can expect in this book and some super interesting facts to get you started

Have you ever been in a situation where you needed to know a piece of trivia, but you did not have the answer? Yeah, I definitely know how that feels as well. The thing with trivia is you only know as much as you have studied and read. So next time you are faced with confusion over the answer to a trivia question, you can be sure that you will be safe because you have the all-encompassing trivia and fact book about all the things that have happened in the world.

There is more than enough information for you to get a great start at learning extensive amounts of trivia. If you are looking for a specific genre of trivia, then you can simply locate the chapter that you need and start there. Impress your friends the next time that they ask the most random trivia question. Surprise them with your knowledge and expertise in a variety of subjects.

Some of these facts are even things that you would be shocked to learn. If that is the case, then I am sure others would be shocked to learn them too. Next time you wish to start a conversation with someone but do not know what to say, you will be fine. Simply pull out one of these random facts and start to entertain your friends with the interesting details and things that you have recently learned.

Here are some random interesting facts and trivia to get you started:

Superman Is Super

In the original comic about Superman, he was said to be bald and a super villain that was determined to have the world at his fingertips. He was considered the child prodigy of Professor X and Lex Luthor.

Since the original Superman was only able to leap over buildings such as the Empire State building, he did not have the ability to fly. Yet in 1940, the producer and writer of Superman decided to add in a new feature of flying since the animation for the bent knee jump was difficult to draw.

Hitler Likes To Fart

Hitler liked for everyone to think that he was perfect, so when his medical records were auctioned by the Alexander auction house, they discovered some new information about this perfect specimen history. He had horrible gas issues and would eat over 28 different indigestion pills to cure the problem. The only problem was that these drugs were filled with strychnine, which was poison. This only created liver and kidney issues and did not fix the stomach problems, not one bit.

Let's Work In The Bathroom

Showers may not only be creating proper hygiene but also increasing creativity. Drexel University found that 7 of the 10 people questioned found that they would have more insight as well as ideas for work while in the shower. Some other creativity building activities would include walking and even the act of daydreaming.

You Shall Not Pass

Bees are known for their bites, but humans are not the only ones to have this neck pain (or arm, or leg ...). By protecting their hives from strangers, some "guardian bees" will stay at the entrance and sniff other bees which will come through the entrance. If a bee from another hive tries to steal nectar, the bee will bite and sting the intruder.

Darn Children Questions

The British study recently looked at young children and recorded the questions they asked of adults when around them. It may not be surprising that children go to their mothers for the majority of their answers. They could answer 300 questions a day, one question every two minutes and a half. The mothers said that the most difficult questions they asked were: "Why is the water wet?" and "How shadows are made?

What In The Insect?

You have heard that the number of insects on the planet is higher than people, but it can be difficult to understand what it looks like. Entomologists consider that there are at least one million insects within our planet of which only 1% is the ant population. If you take all these ants (about ten trillion) and put them on one side of a scale that is gigantic, in order to balance that scale, you would need the entire world's population of people (7.4 billion). Yes, the total weight of ants that live within the world is equal to the weight of all people.

Space Perfume

When you see images of astronauts in their suits for space peacefully floating around outside their ships, have you wondered what the scent or aroma of space is? This is not the first question that people have in mind when they think of space exploration. However, according to some of the past astronauts, the atmosphere outside in space gives off a unique smell that does not dissipate when they return to the ship. They described it as "hot metals" or "hot streak".

Goodbye Big Mac

A valley near Volcan in the country Panama is the healthiest place to live in the world. This land, also called Shangri-La Valley, is beautiful with low cost for living expenses, and the life expectancy is significantly longer than the surrounding area. Every region that has healthier people in the world has something in common: a warm climate, a vibrant social scene, a food selection that is healthier, and a slower pace for relieving stress from everyday life.

Lucky It Wasn't A Tuba

The most popular musical instrument in North Korea is considered to be the accordion, and all teachers need to play to get teacher certification. Accordions, unlike grand pianos, are portable and are considered "personal instruments" that can be carried out in the field and played for the workers within the field.

Good Dog

In the trenches of the First World War, the US Infantry Division could not communicate with other troops because grenades had damaged the telephone cables. A young private citizen had a unique solution. Rags, a crossbreed terrier whom the soldiers had adopted in Paris, carried the messages from one department to another, which he put in his collar. He saved many lives and when Rags died - in Maryland, at the age of 20 - he was buried with military honors.

Iron Man

Iron is an important nutrient for the human body. Iron deficiency can be associated with fatigue because red blood cells help deliver the oxygen needed for energy production in the body. Surprisingly, a healthy adult has lots of iron in his body and can pull out and melt to make a 3-inch-long nail.

Broccoli… What?

McDonald's once created broccoli flavored-like bubblegum.

Zombie Is Real

A fungus will create a zombie then control the minds of the host. Ophiocordyceps, the tropical fungus, infects the central nervous system of ants. When fungi stay in insects for 9 days, they can completely control the activity of the host. They force the ants to climb the tree, curl up, fall into the cool, moist soil, and the mushrooms thrive. There the mushrooms wait for the sunrise to force the antenna to bite the leaves and kill them.

Hawking Is The Real King

Stephen Hawking was said to have been dead by age 20 by his doctors, however, even though he had ALS, which usually kills you in months, he lived to be 76 years old.

Hawking was said to place bets on scientific theories that eventually were found to be false, resulting in him losing the bets. One such bet was that no one would ever discover the Higgs boson, however, he lost this bet and lost $100.

His colleagues once thought Hawking was crazy and that his theory about black holes was rubbish. One of the rubbish theories that he had was the theoretical discovery that black holes would radiate.

Hawking wrote 5 children's books with his daughter Lucy. Each one focused on a boy named George. George had traveled around the world including the universe.

Armageddon Is False

NASA is showing the film, Armageddon, during the management training program. The task of the new leaders is to discover as many mistakes as possible. At least one hundred and sixty-eight were found.

Aliens Aliens

Steven Spielberg wanted to use one of John Sayles' scripts that he wrote called Night Skies. However, the script was about a family who was attacked by aliens that visited Earth. Instead, he developed the E. T film and made it one that all the people in the family could enjoy. Sayles was not the scriptwriter on that one. However, Spielberg decided to hold on to the script for the scary one to later produce as Poltergeist.

We Hate Clowns

For the 1978 film of Halloween, the budget was pretty tight, so they took a clown head and a Captain Kirk mask, used paint and painted it white, and the actor who played the villain walked around in that mask. This worked out in the end for them and was a huge success.

Better Than Musical

Sopranos is one of the most famous and respected TV series of all time. The show brought HBO on the map and was the first sign for the audience that HBO had crossed the limits of its television series as a network. The HBO leaders, however, decided to include the weapon in the "R" of the Sopranos logo to ensure that the audience realized that this was a TV series about gangsters. At first, they were afraid if they did not make it clear that people would see the Sopranos ads and would think it was a music series.

Earth Hour Please

The St. Isaac's Cathedral in St. Petersburg is the largest Orthodox cathedral in the city and among the largest cathedrals in the world, but did you know that this beautiful cathedral rests on 10,000 tree trunks? They are sunk in the marshy terrain below.

Closer To Heavens

The name of Meteora means "floating in the air" and we bet you can see why? The monasteries were built centuries ago on the rocks of Meteora. Today there are only six. The monks live in four Eastern Orthodox monasteries, while the nuns live in the other two.

Chapter 2: Places

The only island with a railroad is Cuba.

There are 46 European countries with the largest of them all being Ukraine.

Scotland is the only location that has 790 islands. These islands include a group that is called the Shetland, the Hebrides, as well as the Orkney.

Wanlickhead is the highest elevated location in Scotland, as opposed to what many believe as the Highlands.

Scotland Whiskey is the most bought and looked for whiskey. It is also the national beverage for the country for the past few centuries.

What is the official animal of Scotland? The unicorn.

What is Scotland most famous for? The Loch Ness monster and its freshwater lakes. The Loch Ness monster resides in their most famous lake, the Loch Ness.

The bank located in the United Kingdom is the oldest Bank of Scotland that has survived since the 1695 time period.

The Nile river is the longest river to pass through Egypt. Cleopatra was said to sail down the Nile river.

Contrary to popular belief, the workers that built the Pyramids were in fact not slaves but paid architects.

If you are looking for the majority of the Pyramids, then look no further than the West bank of the Nile River.

What is the largest pyramid, which is located in Egypt, made of? It is made of 2 million 2 ½ ton bricks that are stacked on top of each other. These bricks were made of hard stone.

Over the span of 80 years, it took the express help of 20-30,000 workers to build what is now called the Giza Pyramid.

In spite of the enormous external heat, the temperature level in the Pyramids will stay relatively constant at a temperature of 20 centigrade.

Since the Pharaohs were so treasured, the Pyramids became their tombs when they would pass on. In fact, some of the most famous ones are King Tut's tomb and Nefertiti.

There are roughly about 200+ languages that are spoken within the European continent.

Disneyland, which is located in Paris, is said to be the most visited of all the tourist locations in Europe.

The average lifespan of an ancient Egyptian was around 30 years old. The ancient Egyptians lived about 3000 years before us.

Many people think of Cleopatra as an Egyptian. However, she was actually Greek. She was also the last Pharaoh of Egypt.

In the 1800s, the children were given medication that contained Morphine. This was found in Mrs. Winslow's syrup for soothing.

What is one tradition that Egypt has? The exchange of the alliances.

Although Giza Pyramids are considered the oldest out of all of the 7 Wonders of The World, they are still standing and can be visited by tourists.

What lasted 200 years in Pisa and is still in effect today? The Torre Continua

The largest island in the world is what? Greenland

Switzerland prohibits night outings in the toilets. They also discourage the flushing of toilets after a specific time due to noise regulations.

Which country has a yearly contest that judges the ability of a husband to carry his wife for distance and length? Finland Many scientists believe that the Mediterranean was once dried out for over 600,000 years making it a desert.

How did Europe get its name? In the Greek myth about the Phoenician Princess, Europe, Zeus took off and disappeared to Crete. Europe took over as ruler and thus, we get the name Europe.

Shwedagon Pagoda is a golden pagoda that has 5,448 diamonds covering the pagoda along with 2,317 inlaid rubies. The top of the pagoda is made of 76 carats of diamonds.

Berlin is the world's leading art capital. The city's famous East Side Gallery is 1.3 km. from the Berlin Wall. It has 105 paintings by artists from all over the world. At the same time, the City National Art Museum was opened in 2017 and is the largest street art museum in the world.

In Mumbai, dabbawalla is people who provide hot meals from houses and restaurants to employees. They offer more than 200,000 lunch boxes every day. The service dates back to 1890.

The bridge Lisbon located at 25 de Abril is known to have the longest span that is centrally located. This is done by suspension making it longer than any other Bridge in Europe as well as the Golden Gate located in San Francisco. The suspension equipment is in the same color scheme as the Golden Gate Bridge which makes it easy to compare the two. The only difference is the company which built the bridges.

Which country is the father of the Olympics? Greece, however, the first time they celebrated Olympics was in 776 BC, and the first modern-style Olympics took place in 1896. The next time the Olympics were held in Greece in 2004.

The Marshall Islands in the Pacific are the most vulnerable island states and pose the greatest risk of flooding due to climate change.

Prince Philip, a British Queen's husband, respects the local people of Johannin on the island of Tana in Vanuatu. Supporters of the Prince Philip movement believe that the Duke is the descendant of one of his spiritual predecessors and that he will visit them in 2016 - if they are lucky - they will calm down.

In French Polynesia, Atom Tematangi is anti-Makkah. This means that Muslims who wish to pray on the island can bow and face in any direction because they will theoretically face Mecca.

Which two animals make their home in Africa? Giraffe and the elephant

There are hundreds of playgrounds for older people at Barcelona. The spaces promote fitness and reduce loneliness in elderly citizens.

Lead miners in Wisconsin would spend time burrowed into hills, and this is the reason that it is called the Badger.

Nauru has the largest overweight population in the world with over 95% of them being overweight. However, there is no McDonald's there.

Which countries would Africa be larger than:

- Mexico

- Most of Europe
- China
- USA
- India

This makes Africa second largest on the country scale.

There are three places that are very dull in their names. They are the league of extraordinary communities.

- Boring, Oregon
- Bland Shire, Australia
- Dull, Scotland

Pompeii shows evidence of takeout restaurants being present.

The road on route 66 has rumble strips when driven at the right speed will play "America the Beautiful."

Topeka, Kansas renamed itself Topikachu in 1998. This marked the US debut for Pokémon.

Atlanta has 71 different streets that have Peachtree in the name.

What place in the world has a history that dates beyond the Aztec Empire? The Oxford University is older than the Aztecs.

If Russian cosmonauts by chance landed in Siberia, they would be fully prepared since they carried shotguns for fear of bear attacks.

The Brits and the Japanese view black cats as auspicious. Black cats are given to a bride as a blessing who are married in English Midlands. The Japanese feel that black cats provide good fortune for the single woman.

On Mount Everest, the boiling point of water is a mere 162 degrees, which is around 50 degrees less than the boiling point at the lower level of sea level.

When Melbourne decided to give some trees in their forest an email address, they did so hoping to receive problem reports. They were shocked when they found out they had received love letters.

The city of Portland is only known by this name due to a random coin toss that decided the city's name. If the coin had landed on the opposite side, it would have been Boston instead of Portland.

Which country has the most efficient garbage regulations? Sweden, they only have 1% of their trash in the landfills.

Easter Islands' heads actually have bodies.

There are three cities that are completely surrounded by one other country. Which three countries are these? San Marino, Lesotho, and Vatican City.

Which nation in Africa has never been a European colony? Ethiopia.

Three countries have recognized that UFOs exist.

- Chile

- France

- Italy

The number of Caribbean islands that have been inhabited is <1%.

Which state is the highest and farthest East, North, and West in the US? Alaska

The only state that will enter the Eastern Hemisphere and Western Hemisphere is Alaska.

What sea has no coast and is completely surrounded by ocean currents and is in the middle of the North Atlantic? The Sargasso Sea.

What is the surface that covers this city makes it the largest one in the world? Where is it located? Hulunbuir located in the inner cusp of Mongolia, which is a country within China, has a surface area of 102,000 square feet.

What location lies in both Norway and Sweden? This same place has the shortest location name as well. This location is 'Å'.

What waterway allows the reduction of 8000 miles when traveling from New York to California? The Panama Canal.

The uniforms of the Vatican's guards are designed after whose famous artwork? Michelangelo is the inspiration behind this vividly colored clothing.

What three colors do you see on the Vatican's guards uniforms? Yellow, red, and blue stripes.

There are several waterfalls located all over the world with the 39th being located in Norway. This waterfall is called Seven Sisters and is located near the Fjord at the Geiranger location. It measures 250 meters wide.

What is the one and only natural wonder that can be seen from outer space? The great barrier reef which stretches 2000 km. It is near the coastline of Australia.

Which country has the grandest casino but their law makes gambling illegal for residents? Monaco. However, the workers are allowed to step foot inside the casino and the population is mostly made up of foreign nationals. This means that 80% of their population is allowed to gamble just not natural born residents of Monaco.

Which port is the busiest cruise ship port in the entire world? Miami, Florida holds this record. In 2016, they had over 4.8 million passengers on cruise ships leave from their port.

Where can you see the filming of Game of Thrones and sit on the Throne? Dubrovnik, Croatia. This was the location for the city of King's Landing on the show.

What port was the second location for the Game of Thrones' King's Landing locality? Valletta, Malta.

When did the Greeks learn of Olives? Around 600 BC.

Which mountain contains the highest peaks? The Himalayan Mountains have 19 out of 25 of the highest peaks in the world.

What mountain contains the highest altitude? Mt. Everest holds this record.

What mountain location is said to be located within reach of the moon? Mount Chimborazo holds the record for being in close proximity to the moon. This mountain is located in Ecuador.

Where is the longest chain of mountains on Earth? How long is it? It measures 40,0000 kilometers and is located at the Mid-Atlantic Ridge.

The longest mountain range that is exposed to the world is The Andes Mountains which is 4,349 miles in length.

Where is 70-80% of the water on the Earth stored? The water is stored in the Glaciers.

Where are 99% of the glaciers located in the world? They are located in the Arctic and Antarctic.

What caused the Mississippi River to flow in the opposite direction in two consecutive years in the 1800s? Two distinct 8-point earthquakes were the culprit for 1811 as well as the 1812 reversal of water flow.

Can you name the 7 largest countries within the world?

- Argentina
- USA
- Canada
- Russia
- Australia
- China
- Brazil

These countries encompass more than 50% of the terrain on Earth.

How many bridges does the Trans-Siberian railroad cross? 3,901 bridges are crossed.

Which state is the only one without an official capital on record? Nauru is the only one without a capital.

How many active volcanos are in Japan? 17

One Penn Plaza, as well as several other buildings in the Manhattan area, have their very own zip codes.

Which town in Vermont does not have any McDonald's? Montpelier.

How many rivers are in Saudi Arabia? 0

Which state in the Middle East has no desert? Lebanon.

Chapter 3: People

Who was the first person to become a billionaire simply by selling some books? J.K. Rowling, but she gave away most of the money helping her lose her status as a billionaire.

41% of the children in Africa work in children's sweatshops, especially those between 5 and 14 years of age.

Queen Elizabeth II has owned a slew of corgis, over 30 to be exact, within her lifetime.

Once Reagan was finished with being the President, he was asked to play the Mayor for the town that is portrayed in the movie Back to the Future III. This town was named Hill Valley.

Jeremiah Clarke was an English composer who was very unstable. He decided to flip a coin to see if he should hang himself or drown himself. The coin landed in the mud on its side, so he went home and used his pistol to shoot himself.

What former billionaire gave away 99% of his fortune to underprivileged kids for college? Chuck Feeney is a former billionaire who gave away 99% of his $6.3 billion dollars to underprivileged kids for college. He is now only worth $2 million.

Which continent has the most countries? Africa. It has about 54 separate countries.

South Africa is lovingly named "Rainbow Africa" since it contains several different dialects of languages.

Which location in Africa has a ratio of 1 in 4 for HIV infected residents? Swaziland.

Which country in Africa is labeled with the highest rate of births in the world? Nigeria

Which continent has more natural resources but the least amount of income? Africa. It is also the least developed continent.

What is the number one disease that is killing children in Africa? Malaria, it kills 3000 children per year.

Before Lincoln was a president, he was also a champion of wrestling where he competed over 300 times and won all but one match.

Although Dr. James Naismith has created basketball, he has lost more games than any other coach with the Kansas Jayhawks.

The voice-over actor that plays Winnie the Pooh is Jim Cummings. He uses his voice to contact sick kids that are staying in hospitals to communicate with them.

Where was Winston Churchill's mom born? Brooklyn.

Curious George was smuggled out of Paris by H.A. and Margaret Rey while they fled from Nazis on bicycles.

In 1867, the United States was able to purchase Alaska from the Russians for $72,000,000 dollars.

Apple is so financially sound that they have more money than is held by the US Treasury.

Where do polar bears live? They live in Antarctica although many people believe they live in the Arctic.

There is only 2% of Antarctica that has been able to be explored due to the vast majority of the territory being covered in large chunks of ice. This ice is 1.6 km thick in some spots.

How many Christian-based churches can you locate in Antarctica? 7 to be exact.

In 1977, Argentina hired a pregnant female to travel to Antarctica to claim the continent for them. The child was born on Antarctica which is the South-Eastern Continent.

The highest point in Antarctica is 16,362 feet high. Where is this located? Massif Massif

Which ocean is around Antarctica? The Southern Ocean.

Which two continents do not have mammals? Antarctica and the Antarctic waters.

How many ATMs are located in Antarctica? There is only one single ATM.

What type of fish is located in Antarctica? The fish is frozen fish, and their blood is not able to produce hemoglobin due to the lack of oxygen.

What continent holds 90% of the world's water? The Antarctic.

The largest desert in the world is located where? Antarctica

Due to the climate in the Antarctic, no one is able to live there full time. However, there is a large population of research centers that house up to 1000 research analysts at a time.

Which continent houses the most mental health cases in the World? The US has been identified as having more cases than any other nation.

Which country has the highest divorce rate? The United States

There are about 20 million people in the US that are living in mobile homes.

Which religion holds the place for the second largest religious organization? Judaism

What is the official language of The United States? Nothing, since it is such a diverse community.

On what day does the US see the most sales of condoms? Valentine's day. This makes it a national condom day as well.

The richest person in America is the one that has $10 and no debts. This makes you 25% better off than everyone else.

What document limited the slave trade? The Confederate States Constitution

What is the only location that commercially grows their own coffee? Hawaii

There are 3 states that have towns named as Santa Claus.

Santa Claus, Mohave County, Arizona

Santa Claus, Toombs County, Georgia

Santa Claus, Spencer County, Indiana

How many unmarried women give birth in one year in America? 40%

What percent of the world languages are spoken within the African continent? 30%

Where does half of the diamonds in the world come from? South and Central America

How many users are on Facebook in Africa? 100,000,000

How many Africans are aged 25 and below? 50%

The largest lake in Africa is Lake Victoria. It's a freshwater lake and 2nd largest in the world.

Which country has more pyramids than Egypt? Sudan. It has more than 200.

Which astronaut was allergic to the moon dust? Harrison Schmitt, who was on the Apollo 17 flight.

The book "The Cat in the Hat" took a whole 1 ½ years to write even though Dr. Seuss thought it would only take a week or so.

The inventor of the Pringle can was buried in a can. He died in 2008.

The first year that you have a baby, you will lose 750 hours of sleep.

The tin can was invented in 1810 by the inventor Peter Durand. In 1858, Ezra Warner designed the can opener. From 1810 to 1858, they used a chisel and a hammer to open cans.

The only person to meet JFK, Lee Harvey Oswald, Bobby Kennedy, and Sirhan is Truman Capote.

Fined $100 for voting in the election of 1872, Susan B. Anthony was the first women to vote and not pay her fine.

50 years after the Declaration was signed, Thomas Jefferson and John Adams died in July on the 4th day in the year of 1826.

In 1976, Ronald Wayne, who was the third founder of Apple, sold his 10% share for $800.

The only person to have 2 different Noble Prizes in different subject areas is Marie Curie.

The founder of Wendy's, Dave Thomas, was a high school dropout that earned a GED in 1993. He was voted "Most Likely to Succeed" by his class.

Theodore Roosevelt gave away the bride-to-be for his cousin Franklin Roosevelt's wedding in 1905.

Simon's, from Simon and Schuster's, daughter is Carly Simon.

Although Neil Armstrong did not get his application in on time, his friend slipped the form into the other applications for him. This allowed Armstrong to be on a space voyage.

The yellow peanut M&M is voiced by none other than J.K. Simmons. He has held this title since 1990.

Sumo wrestlers are considered good luck when they make your baby cry in Japan.

Who was the first streetcar conductor to be a female in San Francisco? Maya Angelou.

People have been known to remove rocks from the Petrified forest only to later return it through the mail with an apology note. To remove anything from a national park is a felony and illegal.

Roald Dahl received a report card during grade school that said: "I have never met someone that is persistent on writing the opposite meaning to the word that is intended".

What leader of a country is a trained mechanic? Queen Elizabeth II.

Dolly Parton founded Imagination Library. She founded it in 1995 and has since donated 100 million books to underserved children.

Niels Bohr, the Nobel Prize winner, was given an endless supply of beer that was piped into his home.

In 1998, at the "Coke in Education Day" event that took place in a Georgia school, a kid was suspended for wearing a Pepsi shirt.

The Vikings were known to wear some make-up.

The last known recipient of 2 Medals of Honor is US Marine Kelly, John. He ran towards enemies that were 100 yards in front of him, killed the gunner from the machine gun nest with a grenade while simultaneously shooting another man, and returning to his base command with 8 prisoners. He was only 19 years old.

The 10th President who was born in 1790 still has a grandchild that lives today. He is a direct descendant to John Tyler.

In Canada, Ward Clapham, a Canadian police officer created the positive ticket program. It gives tickets that are positive to those who did a good deed.

A Louisville woman left the bulk of her fortune to Charles Bronson for being her favorite actor. He inherited a $300,000 inheritance for simply being her favorite actor. This took place in 1997.

4 years prior to the ratification of the 19th Amendment, Jeannette Rankin became the first of the female members of Congress. This was in 1916.

The female actress who played Lieutenant Uhura in Star Trek would not have been in any season after season 1 if not for Martin Luther King Jr. When he learned of Nichelle Nichols leaving the show for a Broadway musical, he begged her to stay at Star Trek. He emphasized the movement of civil rights and how she was a pillar to it.

Ray Bradbury, the author of Fahrenheit 451 spent nine days in the UCLA library on a rented typewriter in the basement. He typed out the first draft in those nine days.

Mark Zuckerberg, the founder of Facebook, thought that a voting option to determine the greatness or lack thereof for a post was not a good option for the world. Now it is the most used option on Facebook.

In 1567, a man tripped over his own beard and died. His beard was the longest beard in the world, and it caused him to trip while running from a fire.

A terminally-ill child loved Ghostbusters so much that Dan Aykroyd and Bill Murray downed the Ghostbusters' costumes and visited him in the hospital.

Where did Agatha Christie develop most of her book ideas? She developed most of them in the bathtub while eating apples.

Who invented the Lamborghini? Ferruccio Lamborghini did so to spite Enzo Ferrari when he told him that he may be able to drive a tractor, but he will never drive a Ferrari.

What was the first question that Boris Yeltsin asked Bill Clinton in 1995 when they first met? Do you think O.J. did it?

Warren Buffet has written only one email and he vowed to never write one again since it ended with him going to court. The email was sent to Jeff Raikes of Microsoft.

What was one piece of advice that Alexander the Great offered his men during battle? He told them to shave so that their beards could not be used to grab and attack them.

How many people in the Czech Republic listed their religion as Jedi in 2011? 15 thousand people did this.

What was Dani DeVito's job before acting? He was a hairdresser for dead people.

What did Bill Gates wish to do with his billions when he died? He wished to donate 95% to charity which would total around $77 billion dollars in 2015.

Everyone knows Amelia Earhart flee the first World flight as a woman but did you know that Eleanor Roosevelt was the first "First Lady" to fly with her. They stole a plane during a White House event and went to Baltimore for fun.

Who invented Netflix and why? Reed Hastings invented it due to the late fee he accrued when he rented a VHS of Apollo 13 and they charged him $40.

How did Ella Fitzgerald get her start in Jazz? Marilyn Monroe promised to appear at Charlie Morrison's club every single night that Ella Fitzgerald performed. So, he had her perform nightly. This prompted Ella's career to take off.

Who were the first American women to go to medical school? Elizabeth Blackwell applied to go to Geneva Medical School and the school thought it was a joke and admitted her in 1847. She attended and graduated in 1849 after which she opened her private practice and infirmary that catered to the poor.

Who is the only man that survived both of the bombs on Hiroshima? Tsutomu Yamaguchi is a businessman that during a business trip to Hiroshima was present with the first bomb drop. He was not killed but slightly wounded. He returned to his home in Nagasaki, and the next day he experienced the next bombing and yet again survived. He then lived to be 93.

Many people believe Marilyn Monroe to be a size 12-16 which would be a plus size figure. However, some people believe she was a US size 0.

Chapter 4: Food

What food costs more per each ounce than a filet mignon? Movie Theater Popcorn.

In 1971, Mariano Martinez, a man from Dallas, invented the machine that was capable of making frozen margaritas. He gained inspiration one day when he was at a 7-Eleven. He bought a slushie and thought about how he could incorporate it into a margarita machine. He was only 26 years old.

Moonshiners would wear cow hooves to confuse the police during the prohibition when they went on runs.

How many licks would it take to actually reach the center of a tootsie pop? On average, the tootsie pop would need 364 licks to complete the goal. Perdue built a machine to test the theory.

Dum Dums lollipops have always had a "mystery" flavor. However, none ever knew the flavor combination until now. The mystery is not actually a mystery but a genius way of using left-over supplies. They mix the left-overs of the previous candy with the beginning of the next candy and created the mystery.

Many people do not realize that bananas are berries.

A drink mixture containing rye whiskey, sherry, and rum was chosen to be served to Washington's visitors of Mount Vernon. He called it eggnog.

The toque of a chef holds 100 folds. This is to represent the 100 ways to make an egg.

The lobster was not considered a delicacy in colonial America. In fact, it was extremely cheap since it was abundant, so they served the prisoners lobster.

Reese's Peanut Butter Cups is subsequently named this due to the Hershey's employee who invented the candy. His name was Harry Burnett Reese. This took place in 1920.

The cans of pumpkin in the stores, even ones labeled with 100% pumpkin are actually mixed winter squashes.

In France, it is illegal for the supermarket to waste produce. They have to compost it or donate it to a charitable cause.

Scottish immigrants provided America with Fried Chicken.

WWII thought that tootsie rolls were a great option for the soldiers' rations due to their ability to survive all weather types.

To learn how to make ice cream, Ben and Jerry took a class for $5 that was a distance-style course offered by the Penn State company.

The two decided to only take one course which allowed them to split the training between each of them.

Waffle House is open at all times. So, FEMA uses their index at Waffle House to gauge the severity of a storm.

Guinness estimates that men are losing 93,000 liters of beer each year to their beards. This is especially true in the UK alone.

In 1935, the Hass Avocado became a patent item due to Rudolph Hass applying for a patent. He was a mailman in California.

Frederick the Great issued a proclamation that his subjects should drink beer instead of their morning coffee. This was in 1777.

One of the best brewing companies is Guinness Brewery. They supported the troops that previously worked for them during the WWI time period. They paid them a half wage while they fought and guaranteed to be able to return upon the completion of the war. They went a step further and sent care packages to those that were fighting which contain condensed milk with chocolate.

What is the first prize in the Finland Wife Carrying Competition? The first prize is the weight of your wife in beer.

During the WWII, they used bacon to create an explosive.

What is offered in exchange for donating a pint of blood in Ireland?
A pint of Guinness is given to those who donate. It is said to replace
the iron.

How was Nutella invented? By a pastry chef in Italy. He wanted to
extend his chocolate rations for the WWII efforts, so he mixed
hazelnut with the chocolate, creating Nutella.

Where did the name PEZ come from? It is a Germany word
PffeffErminZ which means Peppermint.

In 1948, the "Chicken of Tomorrow" was nominated and won. This
chicken is now the main family heritage for most of the chicken that
is served today. The genetics are used to dominate the chicken
industry.

Chapter 5: Movies

What was the very last movie to be rented at a Blockbuster? This is the End, and it was rented in Hawaii.

In Titanic, the director drew the picture that Jack is supposedly drawing. Ironically, the picture is of Kat in a swimsuit. However, in the movie it shows her naked.

Steven Seagal got his acting debut in the film Judo which starred him and Gene LaBelle.

Peter Ostrom, who played Charlie from Charlie and Chocolate Factory never played another role. He was a war veteran.

Fox denied the film the Watchmen since they believed it was "one of the most ineligible crap movies that they had read so far that year."

Chris Pratt seems to have stolen his Star-Lord clothing from the series so that he could show in the suites to visit sick children in the hospital who would like to attend Star-Lord.

In Godfather, director Francis Ford Coppola located the cat, that Marlon Brando is holding, in the alley. It was a stray cat that found its way into the movie by pure luck. Brando liked the cat so much that he kept the cat after the movie ended. The cat was so affectionate that the crew thought the noise would mess up shots.

Although 007 from the James Bond movies looked extremely attractive one thing you would be shocked to know is that he was an early balder. He started to go bald at age 17. During the movie, he wore a toupee.

The director of Die Hard took one script that had failed and turned it into a masterpiece. That script was Commando II.

In the movie, Snake on a Plane, Samuel L. Jackson, was tasked with asking the studio and producers to leave the snake on the plane since that was the reason he accepted the role for the movie.

In the remake of Charlie and the Chocolate Factory, Tim Burton had a professional trainer train the 40 squirrels that attacked the kids. He felt it was more realistic than the CGI images that would have looked fake.

Olivia Newton-John had worn pants that were so tight during the last scene of Grease that they broke the zipper during the filming.

What two sounds are used to make the Brachiosaurs sounds in Jurassic Park? The sounds of whales and the sound of snoring.

There are a few distinct differences in the actions of the bad people and the good people in the movie National Treasure. One of those differences is the browser that is used by each team. Nicholas Cage's team used Google to search, whereas the other team used Yahoo for searches.

The movie Django was the first time that Leonardo DiCaprio was not on the top of the billboard for movies.

During the movie Passion of the Christ, the actor Jim Caviezel received a couple of strikes of lightning.

Courtney Love, the widow of Kurt Cobain, believes that the part of the drug dealer in Pulp Fiction was originally offered to her husband.

After the filming of the Cannibal Holocaust, the director had to prove in court that the actors were not injured or killed during the movie.

The director of the Notebook believed Ryan Gosling to be unattractive. That is why he chose him for the Noah part in the movie.

In Slumdog Millionaire, they portrayed the country of India. In one of the shots, Jamal, the main character had to jump into a pile of feces. These feces were produced by mixing peanut butter and chocolate.

To prepare for Peeta, Josh Hutcherson sat down and read the books. The Hunger Games trilogy took him 5 days.

The day after the showing of Top Gun, the navy found that they had an increase in young recruits. This gave them a 500% increase in candidates.

How many pairs of glasses were used during the filming of the Harry Potter series? 160

In order to play the part of a drug criminal in the movie Ferris Bueller's Day off, Charlie Sheen did not sleep for 48 hours prior to filming. This created a dead look that made him seem crazy. .

The movie se7en did not have a lead until 2 days prior to shooting. At that time, they tested Kevin Spacey, and he accepted the role.

When the role of Uma Thurman was over taking drugs, John Travolta had a pin to rejuvenate her. In fact, Travolta pulls out the needle and moves the film backward to reverse the movement.

Who did Christian Bale study to make the character in American Psycho? Tom Cruise was the inspiration.

The actor who played Dracula, Bela Lugosi, passed away years later. When he was buried, he was clothed in full costume garb, including the cape and all.

The writer of Goosebumps wrote the Bazooka Joe comic strips for the wrappers prior to his book.

The actor that played Willy Wonka in the first movie, Gene Wilder, said he had one condition for taking the role. He wanted to limp on his way to the crowd holding a cane, and then fall into a somersault, then jump back up. He said the reason for this was this will establish uncertainty on whether I am lying or telling the truth.

Kids all over the world sent Charles Schultz candy for Charlie Brown after the airing of "It is the Great Pumpkin" show. They all felt sorry for him not receiving candy, so they sent him some.

Disney struggled with the names of the seven dwarfs. They originally thought of:

- Tubby
- Hickey
- Awful
- Chesty
- Wheezy
- Burpy
- Deafy

There are a few Blockbuster stores left. They are located in Oregon and Alaska.

The role of Neo from Matrix was offered to Will Smith. He declined and chose to appear in the Wild Wild West instead.

What was J.K. Rowling doing when she invented the game of Quidditch? J.K. Rowling invented it while sitting in a pub.

Red Dawn, which was released in August of 1984, was the first PG-13 rated movie released with that rating.

Donald Trump was the inspiration behind Biff Tannen in "Back To the Future". This is due to the screenwriter Bob Gale.

How did George Lazenby gain the role of James Bond? He bought a Rolex, a suit, and cut his hair. Then he appeared in front of the producer and lied about his acting credentials. This earned him the lead role in James Bond movies.

Chapter 6: Art

Vincent van Gogh painted his Starry Night while staring out the window of a Saint-Paul de Mausole asylum.

Art used to be the grand event of the Olympics.

Damien Hirst is well known in the British movie industry. He was nicknamed the "Bad boy of Brit Art." Another great accomplishment was his role as director of the "Country House" which is a music video that was sung by Blur Year.

Anish Kapoor, a British art collector, received an award that totaled £350,000 from the courts due to the art storage company that lost an expensive piece of artwork due to them thinking it was rubbish and placing it in the trash.

Piet Mondrian often worked diligently on his paintings until his hands were in an arthritic stuck position. He would then face frustration and madness at his inability to complete the work. Mondrian explained that it is very difficult for others that do not create art to understand why artistic lines can easily become a frustrating thing.

Leonardo da Vinci was a vegetarian that believed in animals' rights to live. He believes this so much that he was often seen buying birds from pet stores. He would then take them outside and set them free.

Leonardo da Vinci left a small sum of 30 paintings that were unfinished. However, he did complete several drawings, as well as sketches and notebooks that were filled with ideas.

Salvador Dali believed that his brother was reincarnated after death.

In each of Dali's paintings, he has a silhouette of his self-portrait hidden somewhere in the background.

Dali has created more than 1,500 pictures, many of which are largely important to the art community. He helped bring the surreal movement to the world.

So, Edgar Degas loved dancing so much that he used it as his inspiration with his artwork. It is estimated that he created over 1500 images that all depicted the dancers in different dance poses.

Paul Gauguin was an architect who worked on the development of the Panama Canal.

Michelangelo painted the murals of the Sistine Chapel. Describes God who gave life to the first man, including the most famous panel, "Adam's Creation." The inventor developed a process of high scaffolding that provided him with the ability to be bracketed to the Sistine Chapel and work on the painting at an up-close view.

John James Audubon was known for painting watercolor. He is created with painting up to 435 watercolors in his lifetime. Audubon was a Caribbean Island-born artist that lived in Santo Domingo in the 1784 time period. He migrated to the US in the year 1802. At this time, he fell in love with birds which prompted his paintings of birds while he lived in the US.

George Braque had the honor of having the first art display to be exhibited at the Louvre.

Da Vinci's 2nd famous painting is housed in a monastery. This image had a depiction of Jesus. However, afterwards, a remodel added a door. The feet were removed to make room for the door.

The marble which was cut eventually to create the masterpiece David by Michelangelo was originally created in 1504. The marble was used from an older piece that had been started 43 years beforehand by Agostino di Duccio, who started it as a statue of Hercules. He left the statue as an installation in Florentine, and it sat for 10 years. Then Antonio Ros Lóine took hold of it but found it to be difficult so he left it for Michelangelo to collect and work on.

Due to all the love letters received, Mona Lisa has her own mailbox at the Louvre.

The color wheel has an invention date earlier than the United States.

Artist Willard Wigan breathed his work. How does he breathe out artwork? This person must have huge exhales. Not completely. Wigan's work is "micro-sculpture". They are small and must be seen under a microscope. By doing his art, Wigan has to slow down his heart rate and work between impulses. The work he inspired was Alice from Alice in Wonderland, but his performance was better in the remake.

Banksy has been making art for a while. His most expensive piece was sold at an auction for 102,000 pounds. It depicted the image called Bombing Middle England. In 2008, Banksy visited Louisiana after Hurricane Katrina struck. After that, he left some pieces on walls in Bethlehem and West Bank.

To obtain higher performance levels in reading as well as math, what do you need to do? Learn about how to create art.

Recent research studies on the brain have shown that creativity promotes social development and self-esteem.

Painting the lips of the Mona Lisa was such a task that it took the famous artist, Leonardo da Vinci, 12 years to get it just right. That is just the lips portion of the painting. Imagine how long the rest of the painting took.

In ancient Rome, the statues were made with heads that would detach. This made it easy to remove the heads and reattach them with other bodies.

Picasso was able to draw before learning to walk. The first thing that he said which was uttered to his mom in Spanish. It was the word for pencil.

There are several ways that you can interpret the world. Children utilize art to experience the world through the perspectives of the other people within the world.

Art provides the perfect resource for learning that is fun while playing with different mediums.

Art is able to teach us how to solve problems which will teach us logic and reason. It enables us to find the solutions that others would not find.

Pablo Picasso loved animals so much that he owned a pet monkey as well as an owl, goat, turtle, and a few cats and dogs.

What can you develop through art? Imagination as well as critical thinking.

Everyone has that creative bone in them when they are born. It may take some of us longer to connect with it, but it is there. Some just need more practice to find their creativity.

What was invented in England in 1565? The very first pencil.

To learn to be creative, you must utilize your learning skills like you would learn how to read. You also need to learn creativity like writing. It is a deliberate act of learning that is used to process these actions.

Chapter 7: Animals

What are the largest living lizards on the Earth? The Komodo Dragon which originates from Indonesia.

Owning only one guinea pig is illegal in Switzerland.

How big was the largest Komodo Dragon? 10.3 feet in length from head to the tip of the tail. It weighed 366 lbs.

In 1982, the ratio of sheep to the population in New Zealand reached a record of 22 sheep per person. Today, this proportion has fallen sharply. According to the January 2017 report, New Zealand is home to 27.6 million sheep - about 6 per person.

In 2016, Ludvine the bloodhound ran in a half marathon that was 13.1 miles. This was located in Alabama. The dog finished in 7th place.

Chihuahuas, although they have a small-sized body, have the largest brains, due to comparison with their body stature to the brain.

A grumble is a group of pug dogs.

Prior to mating, the female giraffe will share her pee with the male giraffe by peeing in his mouth.

The feet of a Gecko have a sliming effect that can be turned off and on when they feel like it.

Trained dolphins are defending the US Navy base near Seattle that is housing nuclear weapons. This is one of the largest US stockpiles of weapons that are nuclear.

Ants can sometimes misinterpret the smells of the scent trail and will break off and walk in circles. They can eventually get others to join and if enough joined, they will create a death spiral.

A goat's pupil is actually rectangular.

Although many people believe the flamingos bend in their leg is a knee, it's actually an ankle.

Do you think your dog can understand you? Well, you are likely to be right. They can understand 250 gestures as well as words. Dogs have the intelligence of a 2-year-old.

The only animal that is known to blush is the human.

Dogs have been named in wills as primary beneficiary in the US. There are at least 1 million rich pups.

In WWI, a black bear was adopted by a Canadian soldier, who named the bear, Winnipeg. Winnie resided at the London Zoological Gardens, where everyone loved her. A boy named Christopher Robin loved her so much that his father started to author stories about the boy and the bear. A.A. Milne was the writer of Winnie the Pooh. The boy named his own teddy after the bear in the zoo.

The only bird to communicate with infectious laughter is the Kea parrot. They warble when hanging out with other birds as well as the times that they are in a good mood. Although they are not mammals, they can do this action, ironically.

Are cats allergic to humans? Yes, some are.

What animal has cubed shaped poop? Wombats.

Dogs have corn chip smelling feet, that is where the term Frito feet comes from.

What animal has blue eyes during the winter and gold eyes during the summer? The Reindeer.

There is a bird that is called upon by humans to assist them with locating bees nests. This bird is the Honey Hunters. They are located in Mozambique and they use a call that is special to them for aiding as a honeyguide. The bird will get the left-over beeswax.

A blue whale that is newborn will gain 200 lbs. per day during the 1st year of life.

What is a baby porcupine called? Porcupettes.

What animal have many aquatic aquariums tried to keep in captivity but failed to do so? The Great White Shark. This is due to the electricity interfering with the electro-sensory systems that help them survive.

What one animal can withstand the bite of a scorpion? The grasshopper mice who turns the venom into pain medicine. They are now preying on scorpions.

The butterfly that has clear wings and can be transparent to avoid predators is called the Glass-Winged Butterfly.

What do white-faced capuchin monkeys do when they meet as a greeting? They stick a finger in the other monkeys' nose. This is their way of saying hello.

What anthropoid can be frozen for 24 hours and then thawed in the sun and walk away unharmed? The Scorpion.

Wojtek is the bear that was initiated into the Polish Army during WWII. He carried ammunition to troops and drank beers with them.

Due to the finding of penguin bones on Seymour Island, scientists have identified that the penguin was 6 ft tall and 250 lbs. 37-40 million years ago.

What another animal, when held in captivity, can learn to talk? The Raven is said to learn to talk better than a parrot.

What is the ratio of ants to humans on Earth? 1.6 million per person.

Chapter 8: Television

Why did Mr. Rogers announce to the viewers when he was feeding the goldfish? One of his viewers was blind and she wrote him a note to ask for him to inform the viewers when he feeds the fish. She wanted to know the fish was still alive.

Before Miley Cyrus became famous for her dancing act with Robin Thicke, she launched her career on Disney's television show, Hannah Montana. In this television series, actor Jason Earles played the character of Jackson, Miley's older brother. However, what is interesting is the age of Earles. Earles was 30 when Hannah Montana started. By the end of the television series in 2011, he was 35 years old, more than 15 years older compared to the character Jackson.

MTV began broadcasting on August 1, 1981, "Ladies and gentlemen, rock and roll". The first video jockey once described MTV with these words, "The best TV combined with the best radio." The music network featured their first song by the Bugles' "Video Killed the Radio Star".

Late Show of Ireland that started to air in 1962 and The Tonight Show, which began in 1954, are the world's longest television shows.

In 2002, Steven Spielberg was able to finally finish the university studies he had started years before. It took him 33 years to get back to school and graduate. Spielberg used his Schindlers list to get an example of student life.

Throughout his career in the first television series, actor Matt LeBlanc, who played the character of Joey Tribbiani, was extraordinarily strong. He was starting to turn gray in the first season of the show.

Hugo, directed by Martin Scorsese, was the first film that this director directed without including Leonardo DiCaprio in the film in 12 years.

Pierce Brosnan is not allowed to do any of his moves that were coined during the James Bond films. He has been banned from doing those moves since 1995-2002.

Director David Fincher thought that the Starbucks stores in each LA neighborhoods in the late 90s were "super good stores", so he developed the Fight Club coffee chain for his movie. He asked for permission to have a Starbucks cup in each scene in the movie. The only exception was that they did not accept his proposal so he used Graffito coffee instead.

Walt Disney did not feel Alfred Hitchcock was a good option for the Disney name and refused his proposal to make a film at Disneyland. This took place in the early 60s. The reason Disney stated was due to the disgusting Psycho movie that Hitchcock had previously produced.

In 1985, The Soviets created their version of the Hobbit. This movie is visible on YouTube and is really an interesting movie to watch.

To get the Mickey Mouse voice correctly, they joined together the voice of Mickey and Minnie from the 1930s.

The first tape recorder was marketed for consumers to purchase in the United Kingdom in 1963. This record had a maximum record time of 20 minutes for television shows. Sony launched one of the first programs for home videos two years later. However, it took 10 more years for the VCR to become accepted as a household name.

C.K. - This is a true TV artist. He is known to write or work on every aspect of the TV series Louis, but he does all the adventures with his camera, perfect creativity and complete television production freedom.

Jack's role in the Fox TV show was written by Matthew Fox. The player told Michael Keaton to play Jack who was planning to kill the wrong pilot. The series is more focused on Kate and her other servers.

The 1938 model television could be found for a 12-inch screen for $445. In today's price, it would be more than $7200 dollars for the same-sized TV.

Bulova watches filmed and aired their first commercial in July of 1942. It was filmed in New York and aired prior to the baseball's game between Brooklyn and Philadelphia. Each ad cost the company $9. The very first TV advertisement was done by Chevrolet, and it aired in June of 1946. The company paid $9 per ad.

Two days prior to the British war being declared with Germany, the BBC came under tension. A cartoon by Mickey Mouse was the last thing aired.

The first non-aired channel that depicted the child with a blackboard and a toy as the dead air screen, was aired in 1967 and it lasted till 1998. This took place on the BBC channels. This was a test card that would show the channel was off. Then the channel was returned in 2009 with HD capabilities.

Philo Farnsworth, which is the creator of the electronic TV, was in fact not someone that used a TV ever.

Although TV is a no longer a luxury by today's standards, it is still a small investment. In 2012, a 152-inch television was released that would cost the buyer 60,000 Euros. The developer of the TV was Panasonic.

The original use of HD TV was in Britain when the revolutionary TV was produced with 405-line programming. This launched in 1936. Its quality was not as high as our current HD but for the time, it was HD to them.

It is estimated that children see about 11,000 murders committed on a television show before the age of 14 years old. At age 18, the number of murders seen on TV is increased to 200,000.

99% of American homes are adapted with at least one TV in their home and 66% have 3 TVs in their home. More than half of those are paying for local cable channels.

Americans are viewing around 250 billion hours of television each year.

The average 65-year-old man has potentially seen over 2 million TV commercials during his lifetime.

The 1960s was the generation that brought us the television. The first television satellites were able to be launched in 1962 and then again in 1969. These broadcasted to more than 600,000,000 people who watched TV from their homes.

The first online television series of 200,000 lines had a moderate picture capacity.

It is estimated that on January 14, 1973, about 1 billion people watched Elvis Presley's life in Hawaii.

The Daily Mail ad was aired on 1978 by actor John Logie Baird. He viewed it on the first color TV to be shown in public in the town of London.

In the 1941, Brooklyn Dodgers and the Philadelphia Phillies, the first TV commercial was broadcast for 20 seconds. This is a watch made by Bulova.

Most popular and watched television shows:

- (105.9 m) M * A * S * H
- (52.5 m) Friends
- (80.4 m) Cheers
- (50.7 m) Magnum PI
- (76.3 m) Seinfeld

Studies show that between 2006 and 2007, only 18% of unpopular TVs were recycled. About 82% are end up in landfills which generates many harmful electronic wastes.

Where do more people watch television - TV or smartphone? Smartphone.

How many hours a day do American families watch TV? 8 hours per day.

How many TV sets are there in the American households? 275 million or more.

How much do American households spend on their TVs on average? 4%.

Advertising was not always expensive. In 1941, the 20-second prime time broadcast time was worth $9. Today, during the halftime break of the Super Bowl, the price can reach $2.7 million for 30 seconds.

The Russian scientist Constantine Pers invented the word "television" in 1900.

What year was the first TV station started in the US? 1928.

After WWII, the TV became so much more popular and mainstream. By 1948, there were 1,000,000 televisions in homes.

Peppa Pig aired a show that taught kids that they did not need to fear spiders. This episode was pulled from the Australian channels due to the real spider concern they have there.

Cookie Monster was reported as changing his name. However, he did not change his name. In an episode of 2012, he said, "We need to stop this rumor from Veggie Monster before my reputation is ruined."

Chapter 9: Music

In the 5th and 6th century, those in England, as well as Scotland, would throw some pithy and witty verses that were insulting. These were the first rap battles to take place. It was called flyting.

The oldest piano was built by Bartolomeo Cristofori who was Italian. It was built in 1720. It is located in New York City at the Museum of Art.

Gloucestershire UK airport utilizes Tina Turner's music as a way to scare away birds from the airport runway. Her songs are played all day and night to block the birds' wishes of coming to the tarmac.

Axl Rose is such a unique name since its anagram is oral sex. This is William Bailey's stage name for Guns N' Roses.

Termites really love to listen to rock. As per an Australian study, they found that termites will eat more wood when exposed to rock music. The vibrations that are sent through the wood encourages the termites to increase their feeding frenzy.

Where does the longest national anthem hail from? Greece has an anthem that is 158 couplets.

Music is able to reduce the effects of chronic pain, as well as relieve the effects of depression. This will react with your body as well as your soul. It will increase your heart rate for a healthy life.

Through numerous studies, the French have determined that loud music can stimulate more drinking. In restaurants, you will hear louder music during the peak drinking times to increase sales. If you play slower music, it can take 15 minutes to finish a drink. However, if you play faster and louder music, it can take as little as 12 minutes to finish the drink. As we already suspected, according to a French study, loud music stimulates drinking.

The jackhammer produces a volume of 120dB. Manowar had no problem with reaching this goal. To make its debut at the 2008 Magic Circle, the Heavy Metals band developed an additional special amplifier that could produce a spectacular decibel rating of 139 decibels out into the audience's zone. This beat the jackhammers' noise level.

We all know that Leo Fender is the famous inventor of Fender legendary electric guitars. His most popular model the Fender Stratocaster is still the most famously-used guitar in the world. Fender made history for musically-inclined individuals by creating these guitars. Ironically, Leo is unable to play the guitar himself.

Music has been shown to activate the nucleus acumens in the brain. This will trigger the dopamine, which is the chemical compound you get when you eat or have sex. That means that music can trigger similar effects as sex.

Listening to music during work can dramatically improve your performance.

Music has also been said to improve the immune system for adults.

There are few activities in life that use the whole brain and music is one of them.

The main cause of goosebumps is when you listen to music, it releases the dopamine in the brain with the expected peak of the song.

Scientists have discovered that Wannabe, a song by the Spice Girls is an unforgettable song because people knew it within 2.3 seconds, well below the average speed it takes to recognize the song of 5 seconds.

Regular music production will physically change your brain structure.

Music reactions in the brain are the same as when eating your favorite foods.

After the famous musical group, OutKast produced the catchy song "Shake it like a Polaroid". The Polaroid company contacted the press and released a statement informing the world that shaking your picture would damage it.

When Aqua came out with their Barbie girl song, Mattel tried to sue them for using the name. The judge found the case pointless and told Mattel to "Chill."

Elvis Presley had an inventive manager. He made "I hate Elvis" buttons to sell to those that did not buy his records. This ensured he was still getting their money.

Chapter 10: Random

Bubble wrap had another intended purpose when invented. What was that purpose? To be used as 3D wallpaper.

The first national color television program in France was the 1954 Roses Tournament Parade, but most of the programs were in black and white until 1965. The sale of color television sets in 1972 exceeded the blank sets and black for the first time.

There was a crazy man running loose in London in the 1600s. He would spank his victims with a rod and yell out "spanko" then run off.

The percentage of Denmark Jewish people that survived the Holocaust was 99% despite Hitler's efforts to annihilate them.

You can know the temperature by counting the sounds of cricket!

Sandstorms swallow entire cities.

The land that connects from Greenland to Cape Verde is the windiest place on the planet.

A blizzard will make the snow feel like an ice particle hitting your face.

The hurricane in Florida, USA caused 900 captives to escape.

When the flood came, the worms squirmed up from the ground.

Hurricanes can drive more than 6 meters of water onto the beach.

In July 2001, there was precipitation in Kerala, India which resembled red blood!

About 2000 thunderstorms are raining on the ground every minute.

The heatwave of 2003 turned the crops of grapes into raisins before they were harvested!

Lightning often follows a volcanic eruption.

The collapse mud down a hillside can carry rocks, trees, vehicles, and entire buildings!

The world's coldest day ever was recorded at -89.2 degrees Celsius. Brrrr!

The unique nature of a heatwave can make railways curve!

Mix wind with dust, and you get a dark storm called a black storm.

Sphenopalatine ganglioneuralgia is the scientific medical term for ice cream headaches.

The Library of Congress receives applications for non-regular books. The most popular is the Presidents' Secrets Book. Although this book does not exist, it was a prop that was used in the 2007 movie called "The National Treasure: The Book of Secrets."

In 1620, The Mayflower landed on Plymouth Rock. One of the journals from the ship read, "We have no time to explore or move further, we are out of food and beer."

The expression bloodcurdling is also a real condition that causes a protein for clotting your bloodstream more due to fear from a scary movie.

Prior to Google's email server, G-mail was on Garfield's website as an email service that was offered for free.

Crayola comes from the French word *craie* and *oleaginous*, meaning chalk oil.

The US Army believed that they could send messages across the room using a telepathic ray gun. This gun was developed in 1998.

The plural form of the word cul-de-sac is culs-de-sac.

The letters et is from the ampersand, which is the Latin word for "and".

Nerf used the slogan, "Nerf you cannot hurt babies or aged people" for their first ad.

Pele was playing in an exhibition match for Soccer in 1967 when the Nigerian Civil War was going on. During his 2 days of playing, the wars stopped to watch him play.

In 1965, it was believed that Americans would have to only work 20 hours per week to live and they would receive 7 weeks that were vacation time.

The Boston Celtics got their name in 1946 when owner Walter Brown chose it above other names such as Olympians, Whirlwinds, and Unicorns.

Bubbles have been known to keep the water in your bath warmer for a longer period of time.

Once a solar eclipse stopped a war in 585 BC due to the Lydians and Medes thinking that this was a sign that the fighting should cease. This took place in Turkey.

Canada thought of renaming the Northwest Territory in the 1990s the name they considered was Bob.

In 2011, Toyota decided to make Prii the plural form of Prius.

The galaxy has been known to have a specific smell. The smell of diesel, barbecue, and gunpowder are the aromatic fragrances that you can smell in space. This is partially due to the dying stars.

The 1908 Olympics had a late arrival by the Russians who were using the calendar that was Julian instead of the calendar that was Gregorian.

The count on Sesame Street loves numbers but this is not a character trait only. In vampire folklore, vampires have a disorder called arithmomania which is a compulsion for counting things.

What tree is the most poisonous tree? The manchineel tree. If you touch it, your skin will burn, if you eat its fruit, you will die, and if the bark is burned near you, you will go blind. It is called the "tree of death".

If you want to clean your brain, then sleep. While you sleep, your cerebrospinal fluid is flushing the brain to wash away the proteins that are harmful and toxic.

When you donate blood in Sweden and it is used, you will receive a thank you text.

Curling is known as the Spirit of Curling due to the good behaviors that are expected by the players. It is expected to be polite and congratulate the other players and abstain from any trash talking.

If you ever get lost in Central Park, just check the lamp posts. They contain a code of numbers. These four numbers tell you the street (first 2 numbers), and the locality (east or west). Even numbers correlate to the east side. Odd numbers correlate to the west side.

The disorder where you buy books and then do not read them is Tsundoku.

In order to contribute to the safety of people in cars, Volvo gave away the patent that they filed in 1962 on the revolutionary three-point harnessed seat belt.

What scientific paper contains absolutely no words? The Journal of Applied Behavior Analysis created a document on unsuccessful ways to treat writer's block.

In Slovak and Slovenian embassies, the staff would meet once a month to exchange the mail that was not correctly marked.

The term jaywalker came from the term Jay being the slang word for a foolish person. That is how jaywalker became known.

The word that describes a word that is its own exact opposite is a contronym. An example would be that you seed the lawn to add grass and seed the tomatoes to remove the seeds.

In 2001, Beaver College changed their name to Arcadia due to internet anti-porn filters that kept blocking access to their page.

To make change for $1, you can try 293 different ways.

The year that Facebook released the newsfeed, Times called it Gen Y's first step to official revolution. Everyone freaked out. This took place in 2006.

Déjà vu is the experience of experiencing an event for the second time. Deja reve is the experience of experiencing a dreamed event.

In Finland, each year they host a Mobile Telephone Throwing World Championship. The most recent winner stated that he practiced by drinking.

A chemical is emitted from grass that is being cut. This is due to distress in the plant for being cut. That is the smell that everyone knows as fresh cut grass.

For less than the price tag of a Ferrari, you can purchase a refurbished and renovated Boeing 727 which can accommodate 23 people.

In 1999, Google offered to sell to Excite for less than $1 million. Excite subsequently turned them down.

In 1913, they had a Gettysburg reunion. Two of the men purchased a hatchet and when they got there, they walked to the regiments site and buried the hatchet.

Play-Doh was initially not a kids' toy. It was invented to clean wallpaper.

For their New Year's ball dropping, Bethlehem, Pennsylvania drops a 200 lb. Peeps chick.

In the Renaissance, they would walk with the ball of their feet first. This was to check for any dangerous debris that could damage their feet. This is due to the shoes being inadequately soled.

The book "Goodnight Moon" was originally refused for admittance into the New York Public Library.

Kinderschema is the trait that many humans adore. It involves small noses, big huge eyes, and a small chin.

During times of war, the troops would set pigs on fire and send them into enemy lines. This was to combat the use of elephants during the war since the elephant did not like the pigs and would run from them.

If you swap out the letters in the word WIZARD with the opposite letter, then it will spell WIZARD backward.

The history of Saint Patrick's Day is loaded with drinking and eating. It was once considered Feast Day, and this was to honor the Christian Saint Patrick. They were allowed to stop being frugal and enjoy the day with food and drink.

What is one thing that murderers never think of when killing someone? That glitter can be used as forensic evidence. Due to its unique characteristics, it can be narrowed down and identify the killer.

In 1948, Mahatma Gandhi died prior to receiving his Noble Peace Prize so that year the committee declined giving it to another person due to his loss. They stated, "There was not a significant replacement candidate that lived."

What is one thing that releases endorphins when done while in pain? Swearing releases endorphins and helps to ease your pain.

In Italy, you can give the Credem Bank parmesan cheese in exchange for cheaper loans. They have a 3-5% interest rate and a fee to ensure the maturity of the cheese. This takes 2 years. If the loan defaults, they sell the cheese. They have 430,000 parmesan cheese wheels and they are valued at $200+ million dollars.

How old was the first person to design the current American flag? He was 17 and it was designed for a school project that received a B-.

How much money is set aside for the US budget for defense? $698 billion which is the combined budget of the next 17 nations.

What can be attributed to the sloppy handwriting of a doctor? The deaths of around 7000 people in each year in the US due to the illegible instructions.

Who decided that two months' salary is the price that a man should pay for the engagement ring? A Da Beers ad campaign told people this.

How much does a cloud typically weigh? 1.1 million pounds.

What is one strange thing that can take place when you have a traumatic brain injury? You may obtain foreign language syndrome.

This syndrome is rare, and it means that you speak your native language in a foreign dialect.

What is one good thing that sarcasm can do for your life? It can promote the creative juices to flow.

Indiana State Legislators worked on passing a bill that would legally define the value of Pi as 3.2 in 1897. It did not pass.

Due to the outrage of some people, the FBI investigated the song "Louie Louie" for dirty lyrics. However, after 3 months, they could not figure out the lyrics and dropped the investigation.

Which military unit had the most decoration during WWII? The unit was the 442nd Infantry Regiment and they were mostly Japanese Americans whose families were in internment camps. They had a motto "Go for broke".

How far would all the blood vessels in your body stretch if removed and stretched end to end? They would stretch around the world more than twice since there are 60,000 miles of blood vessels.

Which one is smaller, the sun or the moon? Due to the proximity of the Earth, the moon is 400x closer but also 400x smaller than the sun, although they look to be the same exact size.

What does the Catholic Church think about the Theory of Evolution? To be virtually certain.

Would you believe that more people suffer bites from the New Yorkers each year than they do by sharks?!

What does the Catholic Church think about the Intelligent Design theory? They believe it is not science even though it has pretended to be just that.

Prior to 1956, the flight paths of planes were not etched in stone. They were allowed to take any route they pleased to get to their destination. They could take the scenic route if they wished. However, when two planes crashed over the Grand Canyon, they changed this rule.

Conclusion

Throughout history, there have been many things that have been invented, many movies that have been filmed, and many television shows shot, but that is not all there is. There were also Presidents, actors, animals, art, candy, food, and even alcohol. With all of this, there is going to be unique and interesting facts and trivia that is sought after. As you read the chapters in this book, you will see how interesting life and the planet can be.

Now that you have read this book, you should know all kinds of things that will help you to impress your friends. These facts cover every single genre that I could think of. With the knowledge that has been placed in this book, you should be able to not only educate your friends but also show them how smart you are and even call them out on the fake facts that they try to use to impress others.

Next time you are trying to impress a girl or boy, you will be able to pull some interesting details out of this book and attract them with your knowledge and random facts.

Connect with us on our Facebook page
www.facebook.com/bluesourceandfriends and stay tuned to our
latest book promotions and free giveaways.

Don't forget to claim your FREE book

https://tinyurl.com/karenbrainteasers